DRAWINGS FROM THE NEWBORN

DRAWINGS FROM THE NEWBORN

Poems and Drawings of Infants in Crisis

By Heather Spears

Ben-Simon Publications

Port Angeles, Washington
Brentwood Bay, British Columbia

Designed by Rita Edwards
Production of Mechanicals by James Bennett
Reproduction Co-ordination by Philip Graham
Editorial Work by Francine Geraci
Printed in Hong Kong by Scanner Art Services Inc., Toronto
Typeset by Dynagraphics

Published simultaneously in the USA and Canada by:

 BEN-SIMON PUBLICATIONS

USA: P.O. Box 2124
      Port Angeles, WA 98362

CANADA: P.O. Box 318
         Brentwood Bay, B.C. V0S 1A0

Library of Congress Catalog Card Number: 85-70771
ISBN 0-919539-02-7

I would like to thank the staff of the neonatal ward
GN, Rigshospitalet, *Copenhagen,*
for their understanding and cooperation,
and the many parents who,
in a time of crisis,
generously gave me permission to draw
their children.

Some of these poems have appeared in *Malahat Review,*
and the drawings have been exhibited extensively in Scandinavia.

For reasons of privacy, no poems in this collection refer to
particular drawings, and no drawing represents or
illustrates any particular poem. Names in the poems are
fictitious, and any resemblance to children of the same
name is inadvertent and coincidental.

For

Lesley

TABLE OF CONTENTS

(Note: Artist numbers listed in the text refer to the chronological order of the drawings' creation.)

Dear parents, sorry

I did not draw your son last night.
When I came by his crib
they had darkened it
with a sheet—"He needs to sleep."
They told me you had looked
among the copies, and then said, "Maybe
she only draws the beautiful ones."

He is beautiful. Despite the shaved head,
the drip and gear. His open eyes
gaze steadily, he sees that he lives.
Two deep lines
at the soft puckered edge of his gown
—beginnings of the red incisions
that cover his neck and chest.
He will heal.
He will sleep all night.
He will not remember the cowled face,
the twin he carried with him out of the dark.
Finished, I tape the sheet in place.
His eyes close, as if by clockwork.

Baby from Sukkertoppen

Flown in haste out of Greenland
and now she lies
in glass as green as ice in snowy whites
that make her skin
almost plum black. How small
is thirteen hundred grams? Her brow
and upper arms so finely haired, her timid breath
that has to be written down to be discerned. She stretches out
a fine formed hand. Maybe happy there, at least less scared
than her mother sleepless on the other ward.

Nadja

It would be impossible to draw her baby
as beautiful as that. The mother
leans against the glass, hours pass.
Her bare arm out of the blue gown
enters, her long hand
strokes and strokes the tiny chest.
It is like a trance. I fail before I start.
Her jealousy is older than this place,
less sterile. Nothing can satisfy. Between that turned head
hidden by long hair, and the minute life
she touches, an absolute.
I sense its rage.
My pencil cringes on the paper.

Gitte

I can hear them talking
behind me, around the one across the aisle:
"I think her time's run out."
"Poor thing." And they manipulate
this switch and that, the instruments clicking
and bleeping. Someone else comes by:
"We'll have to have a christening then,
I could do without that on my shift."
"If she lives, if she lives to morning she's due
for another operation. Have you tried—"
"Digitalis, God yes, everything."
"Try this again, try stepping it up."
They stand and watch the dials, and the faint green
line slipping and running across the screen.

♂ LFV

It's nearly midnight. A man
in a yellow parents' gown stands
motionless beside a box.
Inside the glass
another box, tilted. An unbelievably small
dark red baby with head
fixed between pillows.
I can hardly see its face
for tapes and pipes, the wrist-thick
belly is bound, the hands droop limp
against the cheeks—penis, fingers, toes
doll smooth, slightly unfinished.
The chest looks half transparent. The head, too,
dented under wet hair. Over outrounded closed eyes
long wrinkles draw the brows upward, the flat nose
is pulled askew by the tube.
The father looks up. His eyes, encompassing the room and me,
are still naked with amazement and unsure joy.

Premature

It is less than will.
Dark as blood, so small
she hardly dents this world, withery face that shows
a kind of infinitely pained
acceptance, breath
and heartbeat almost nothing, every shift in pose
a falling to rest, resisting nothing.
The doctor comes to the box, inserts his huge hands.
He talks, touches.
The panel overhead, the three long cords
looped to the bandages, the red
clicking light that enlarges life to readable.
Later, it calls and gleams: a nurse
comes by, calmly taps the glass—"Now, now—"
the clicks resume. This is without will,
or willing to slide into death—but persuadable.

Choice

The place persuades, then,
but the choice is somewhere else, present
but clear of machines and voices, in a space
statistical and pure as mathematics.
The Turk finally leaves, his wife
remains with her blackhaired baby on her lap.
He is large, perhaps unusually relaxed.
Nurses come by, urge her to go to bed.
"It will be good for little Muhammed Ali
when he gets out of this,"
one says, after she is gone.
I can't decipher what is wrong with him
from the card over his crib.
He outweighs the prematures at any rate.
Maybe he will put up a fight.

Parents

"It's different for us—Adam is fine,
only needs to put on weight." His voice
is large with satisfaction. "We don't like to ask
about the sick ones—it must be so hard
for those parents." He goes on to tell
about the one who had the twin
cut out of him.

One week later, and late, I pass
the box where Adam lies: he is being fed.
I say, "Nice Adam's doing well—
he'll soon be going home?"
The doctor's eyes flicker to my face:
"He is only fair." And he stands
absorbed again, pressing the nozzle, the named
child almost covered by his careful hands.

Baby addict

I draw the difficult newborn brow, the whispery line
of the closed eye that lies
like a breath on the surface.
I see nothing special—a shudder that passes.

She was sicker last night. They think
her father's given her mother a fix
in the toilets ("TV SUPERVISED")
—the milk keeps pace.

A doctor tells me what NM means.
"This is the worst there is." Is he making
a judgment? or does this hapless box contain
the longest hurt of all, the hardest parturition?

♀ Hydro-
cephalus obs.

I would not have noticed.
All newborn heads
are large, are tender, are strange.
They could be planets, their form
the most difficult abstract in the world.
What is there to see? She is asleep, her hands
curled at her well formed face.
and now I trace
and retrace the simple profile of that head
from nape to brow, over and over
as if it were changing, its edge
trembling to change, like water swelling towards light.
Even when I get it right, it will not be right.

Oxygen tent

The plastic like stage-prop water
is runny with wrinkled light;
when the doctor throws back the side
it shimmers, its English sign ("NO SMOKING") tilts.
He works fast, his hands
moving in patterns as in a complex dance
his mouth is set
the baby's loud laboured breath
answers his silence, I see how its bandaged head
presses back to accommodate
the metal against its face.
And I know who it is,
in another crib I have drawn
this very child, he was healing then.

Girl twins

Found them eventually
at the far end among the bright machines
and drew the one. She was rigged, but bearably,
coaxed on her side with a pillow to prevent
her pulling from the tube.
I can hardly remember. Only the other one
that my look touched once and leapt from.
Smaller even, mauve as celluloid, her head
hid under the silvery pipes, her body
kept on its back, comfortless.
Between diminutive starved legs
her newbown sex the only detail, piteously declarative.
And the glass box tipped forward, as if presented to me,
in its awful, careful symmetry.

♀ 786 gr.

Yet it was not till the nurse
turned back the flannel for me, and her hands,
suddenly enormous, touched this child
that I knew how small it was,
how even on this page
(8 by 11) I might easily
have drawn it twice its size.
On a spoonshaped bed of fake sheepskin
it swims rather than moves, legs and arms
peripheral, floating, skin across the torso
more like a membrane, alive
with the heart's grape I can nearly see
and whitish pointed bones.
Something is distanced in me.
The fingers stretch like fins, as if they were webbed,
as if it danced a gesture I can't read,
muted and starry.
It has not even learned
to fist, or to return
to the "fetal position"—the simple solace
of the true born.

Kîstat from Greenland

It was a nurse who asked, whose arm
appears across the drawing, the large palm
framing the baby's head. Troll-black,
the spiky hair, right down to the eyebrows, the slack skin
almost blue with anger. Despite her skinniness
"She's doing well, keeps her body heat—"
at four days old, she yells to be held,
quiets when lifted. She's wide awake, her bead sharp eyes
alert, and out of the folded sleeves
of her gown, her scrawny wrists and hands
strike at her mouth with her meek fury: "Little Kîstat."
I left copies for the staff. And one in courtesy
for her mother, who could not live
and was too sick to give me leave.

"Light-child" Sofie RH imm.

The crib with its tucked taut sheet
and curved metal sides
is bluish, brilliant, so the baby's buttery skin
looks almost colourless. Fat and full term,
she sleeps on her belly like a frog, arms and knees
round on each side; ten round toes
show under her vulva with its simple line.
Her rectum's neat as an asterisk.
Only her head is dressed: a slightly
ridiculous gauze cap with a top knot
and bow, and the taped mask.

She lies so quiet I can't guess her breath.
And radiant. In this blond, dim ward
the blue light holds her like a mind, in
its austere, benevolent attention.

Face presentation

The father-love
frightens me less, there is
a kind of spaciousness in it, a displacement
towards rest. Still gowned, he stands
like a child himself inside the door, and shows
two nurses his newborn daughter. Whose lower face
is slurred with purple. "She had a hard fight."
As if the mouth's perfect colour
had leaked outwards over the smooth skin.
Still wet, with threads of black hair
smeared to her airy scalp. And hugged close,
wrapped close. Now he'll walk
to the intensive aisle, and the doctors, there's no haste
with this one—they'll nod, and touch
careful and gentle where she pressed and pressed.

Heart-child's father

His dark thick wrists
hang from the yellow sleeves, the bibbed
pitiful ties at his shoulders.
He leans forward in the chair, his gaze
fixed on the crib, and the one they call
"the big child". His face is erased:
the expressive muscles
utterly soft and lax, it is a nothing-face,
undone, abandoned in its privacy.
The doctor, a woman, bending over the child,
has something to do with her hands.
When at last he stands
to go, he speaks and makes a smile.
He stoops as he passes me, as if he were walking downhill.

Asphyxia

So close, the curtained opening
like a low moon occludes her body:
everything is light.
She has not moved. My face
at level with her face. I draw.
Someone turns her, lays her glossy arm
back across her body. Not a finger moves.
In there, inside the glass,
everything is soft, blurred, warm,
only the nasal tube's blue metal
comes sharp, its shapes
beautiful with utility,
that breathes her so perfectly
her chest does not move. Her closed
eyes do not move.
On the screen, the tiny green snake
of her life whips and whips and whips.

Oesophagus Atresi

For weeks this poem will not write.
I can hear no demand
in his weeping, only hopelessness.
After the scarred cough that wakes him.
I go past.
A nurse has lifted him, lulls him.
The wires to the electrodes
stream from his little limp shirt like banners.
And the milky tube inserted in his belly,
that feeds him.
His eyes are unnaturally black and brilliant.
His fist clenches her thumb.
He sees her, ardently.
Later, back in his crib, he stares
with that same fervour
at the nearest of the plastic picture squares.
His breath chirps over.

†

Any kind
of life is life;
but here, the event cancels all questioning—
the crib, the cold room, the closed door.
Well, the old masters managed,
perhaps casually—after all,
nothing is here. My living eye
flickers without response. My hand,
as if blind, obeys my craft.
Her skin is taut across her face,
the bruises from the drains
look painted on, the long
eye lashes, dark and gold,
lie as if combed. One nostril's
widened. But here
there are no tubes, no life-lines.
The gown and blanket cover what I saw,
which was awful: red, blue, black.
When I went by and could not look,
and was not asked to draw.
Oh child, it should have been then, you had everything
going for you, any kind of life
is life.

SURVIVING TWIN BOY
1984. Pencil on white paper.
24 x 32 cm
Collection Ulla Amsinck, Denmark.
Artist No. 372.

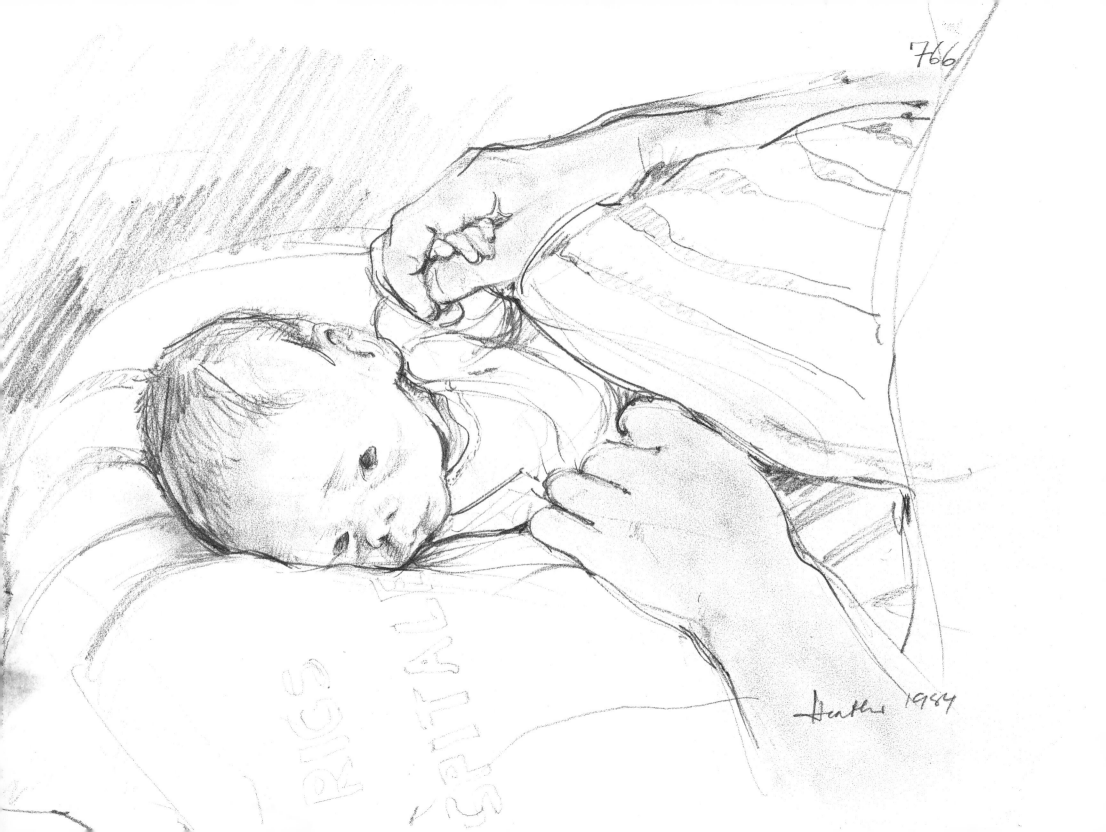

LIGHT-CHILD
1984. Pencil on white paper.
21 x 29.7 cm
Collection Inger Hansen, Denmark.
Artist No. 265

HELGA WITH WALKMAN
1984. Pencil on white paper.
24 x 32 cm
Collection of Dr. Ute Grimrath, Pediatrician, Federal Republic of Germany.
Artist No. 373.

Heath '84

NEWBORN MARCUS
1985. Pencil on white paper.
24 x 32 cm
Collection Mogens Parning and Nia Schulin-Zeuthen, Denmark.
Artist No. 834.

486 fd 21/06

23/06/85

SARAH, *TVILLING A.* BABY IN RESPIRATOR
1984. Pencil on white paper.
24 x 32 cm
Artist No. 371.

TV A
SARAH LFU.

Heather 84

LIGHT-CHILD ♀
1985. Pencil on white paper.
24 x 32 cm
Collection John and Marianne Petersen, Denmark.
Artist No. 559.

OBS.

Heather 9/02/85

LIGHT-CHILD KAREN
1985. Pencil on white paper.
24 x 32 cm
Collection Hanne and Henning Mathiesen, Denmark.
Artist No. 671.

HB
210

Heather 22/03/85

STUDIES OF LIGHT-CHILD MAI
1984. Pencil on white paper.
24 x 32 cm
Artist No. 315.

MAi
716

Heather 84

BABY, *MEC. ASP.*
1983. Pencil on white paper.
21 x 29.7 cm
Collection Mikala Winterø, Denmark.
Artist No. 160.

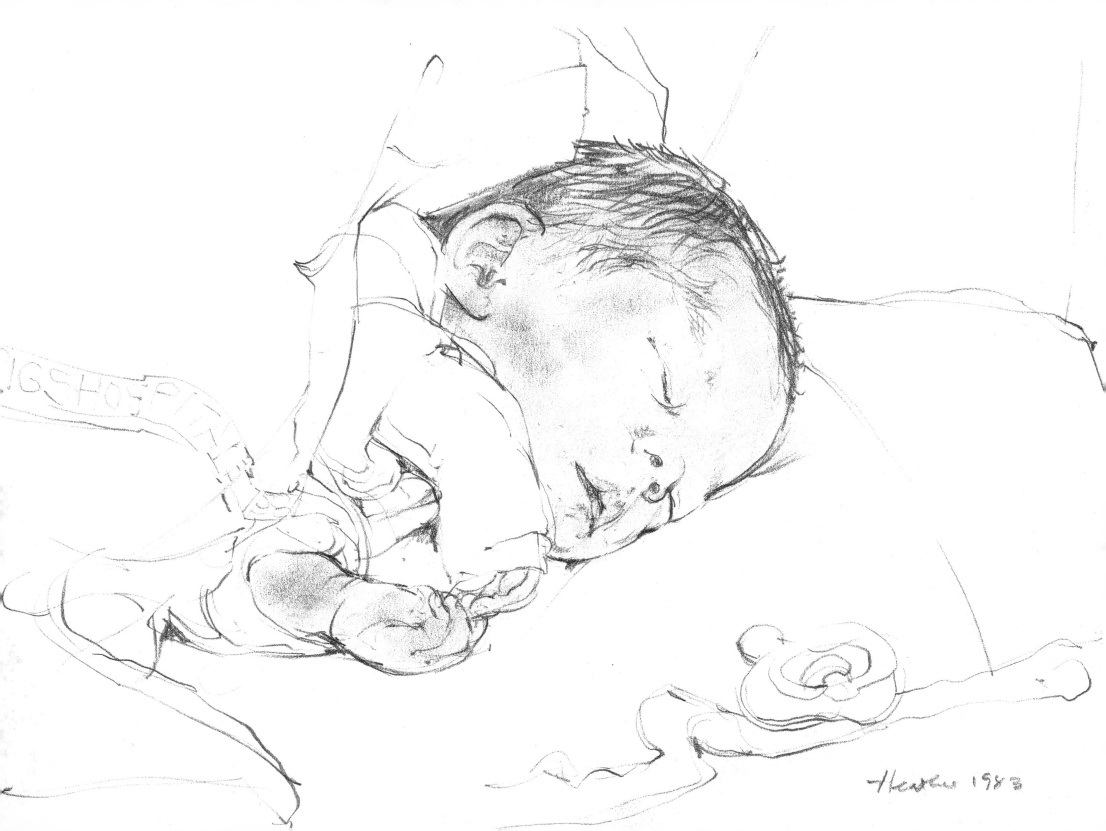

NEWBORN IN INCUBATOR
1984. Pencil on white paper.
24 x 32 cm
Collection Head Nurse Jean-Paul Guilbert, Denmark.
Artist No. 387.

Heather 84

TVILLING A, GREENLAND
1984. Pencil on white paper.
24 x 32 cm
Artist No. 434.

Tv. A
LFV

Heather 84

UNTITLED. MASKED BABY
1984. Pencil on white paper.
24 x 32 cm
Artist No. 235.

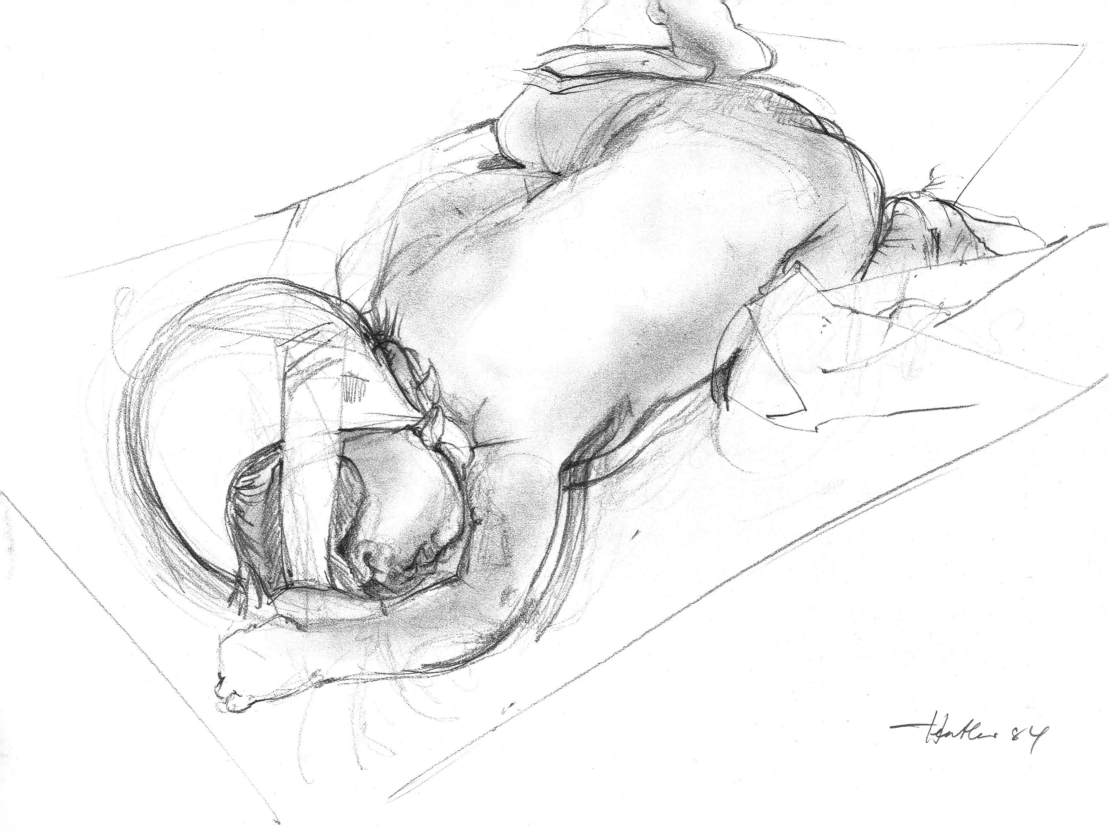

JONAS, *APNOE*
1984. Pencil on white paper.
24 x 32 cm
Collection Karin and Michael Hansen, Denmark.
Artist No. 512.

CHRISTINA, *PNEUMONI*
1984. Pencil on white paper.
24 x 32 cm
Collection Dr. Jørgen Paulin, Denmark.
Artist No. 297.

Heather 22/01/85

Heather 84

NICKI, *PRÆMATUR.* BABY IN A RESPIRATOR
1985. Pencil on white paper.
24 x 32 cm
Artist No. 532.

SIGRID
1985. Pencil on white paper.
24 x 32 cm
Artist No. 535.

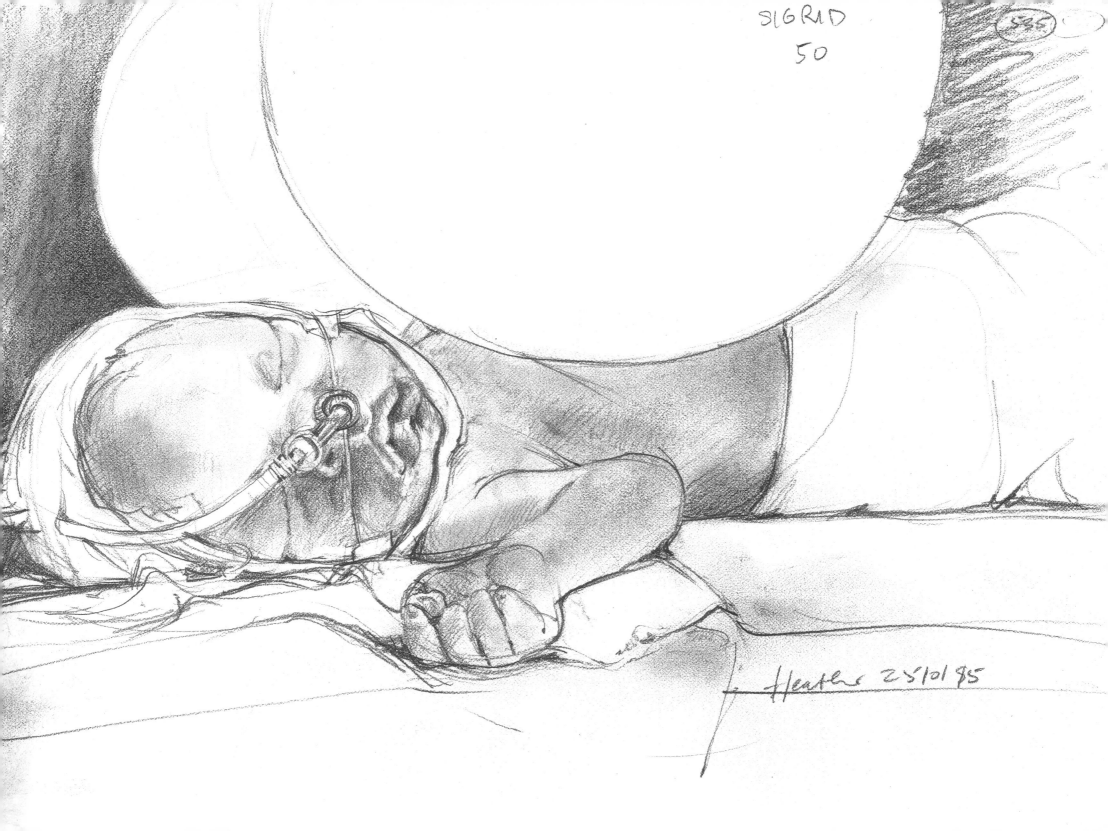

Heather 25/01 85

NICOLAI COMFORTED. INCUBATOR DRAWING
1984. Pencil on white paper.
24 x 32 cm
Collection Beve Tansey and H. David Kirk.
Artist No. 444.

IN HASTE. INCUBATOR DRAWING
1984. Pencil on white paper.
24 x 32 cm
Artist No. 209.

SALINA, 675 grams (birth weight 725 grams)
1984. Pencil on white paper.
24 x 32 cm
Collection Ole Laursen, Denmark.
Artist No. 392.

SABINA
852

SALINA. ENLARGED STUDY OF PREMATURE HEAD
1984. Pencil on white paper.
24 x 32 cm
Artist No. 394.

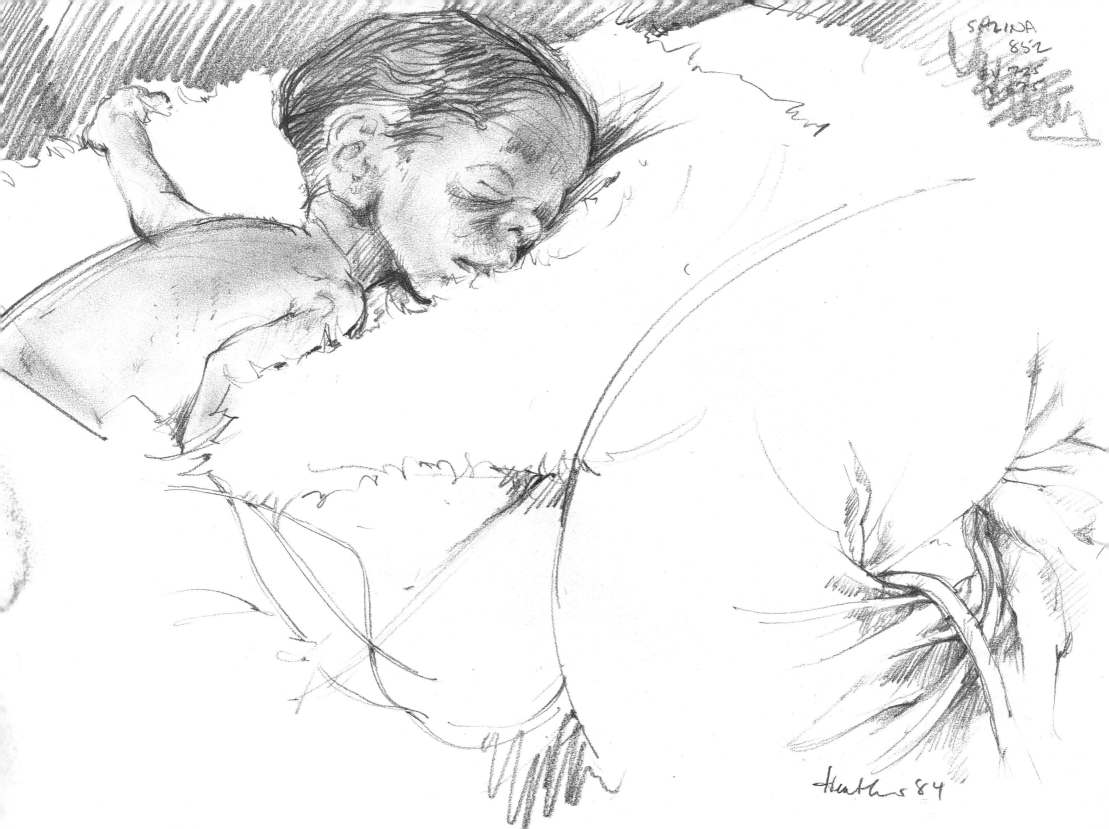

EMIL COMFORTED
1985. Pencil on white paper.
24 x 32 cm
Artist No. 629.

Heather 85

TWO STUDIES, KATYA
1984. Pencil on white paper.
24 x 32 cm
Collection Head Midwife Grete Rud, Denmark.
Artist No. 331.

KATYA
702

Heather 84

NEWBORN LASSE, *DMM*
1985. Pencil on white paper.
24 x 32 cm
Artist No. 492.

Heathens 11/01/85

STUDIES OF MARIA EVA, 640 grams
(birth weight 700 grams).
1985. Pencil on white paper.
24 x 32 cm
Artist No. 790.

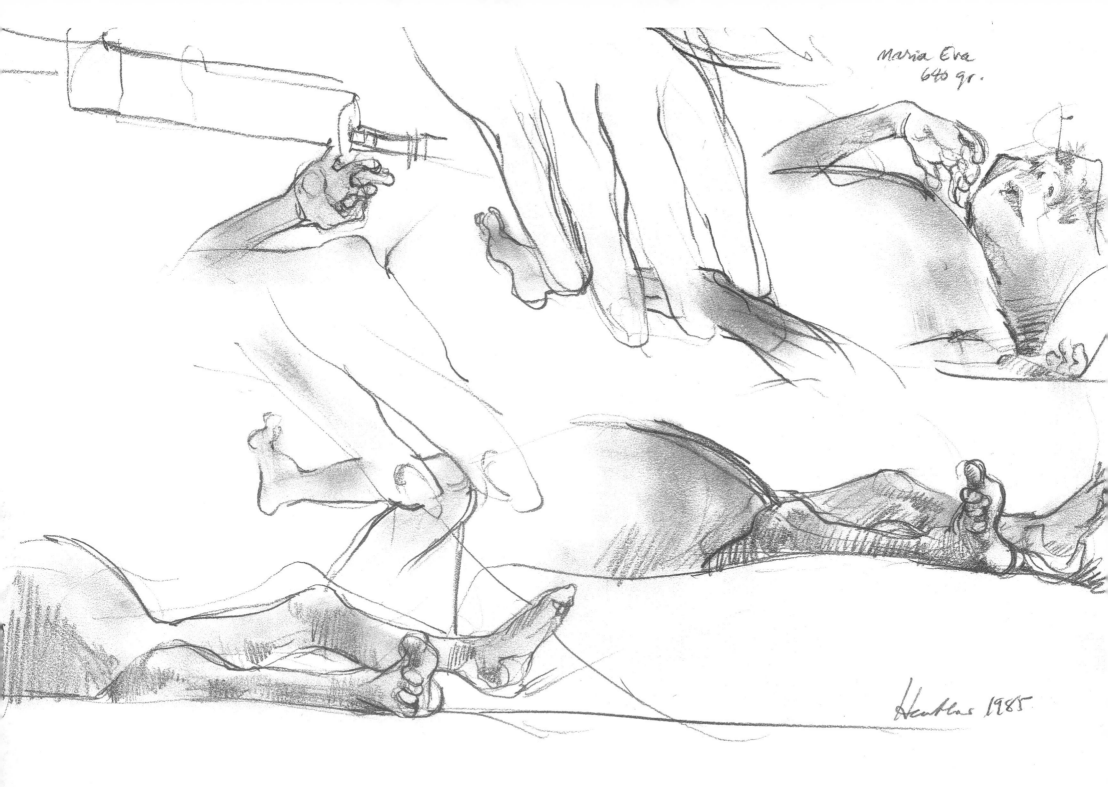

Maria Eva
640 gr.

Heublus 1985

DANIELL (2)
1985. Pencil on white paper.
24 x 32 cm
Artist No. 526.

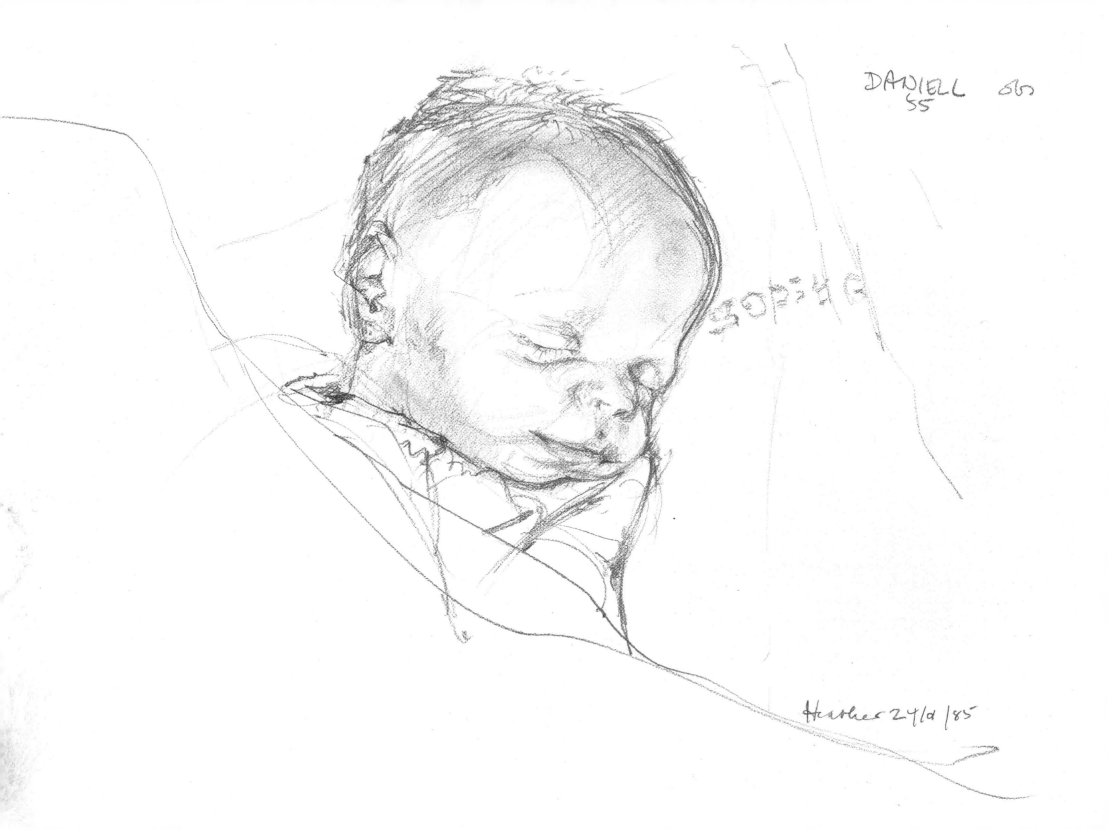

LIGHT-BOX BABY
1984. Pencil on white paper.
21 x 29.7 cm
Artist No. 260.

663

Heather 84

MIA LOUISE, *STENO FALLOT*
1984. Pencil on white paper.
24 x 32 cm
Artist No. 448.

Mia Louise
918

Heather 84

CASPER
1985. Pencil on white paper.
24 x 32 cm
Collection Lisbeth and Claus Rosengaard, Denmark.
Artist No. 759.

CASPER
262

Heather 30/04/85

CHILD, *NM.* HALF-STUDY OF BABY IN BONNET
1984. Pencil on white paper.
24 x 32 cm
Artist No. 379.

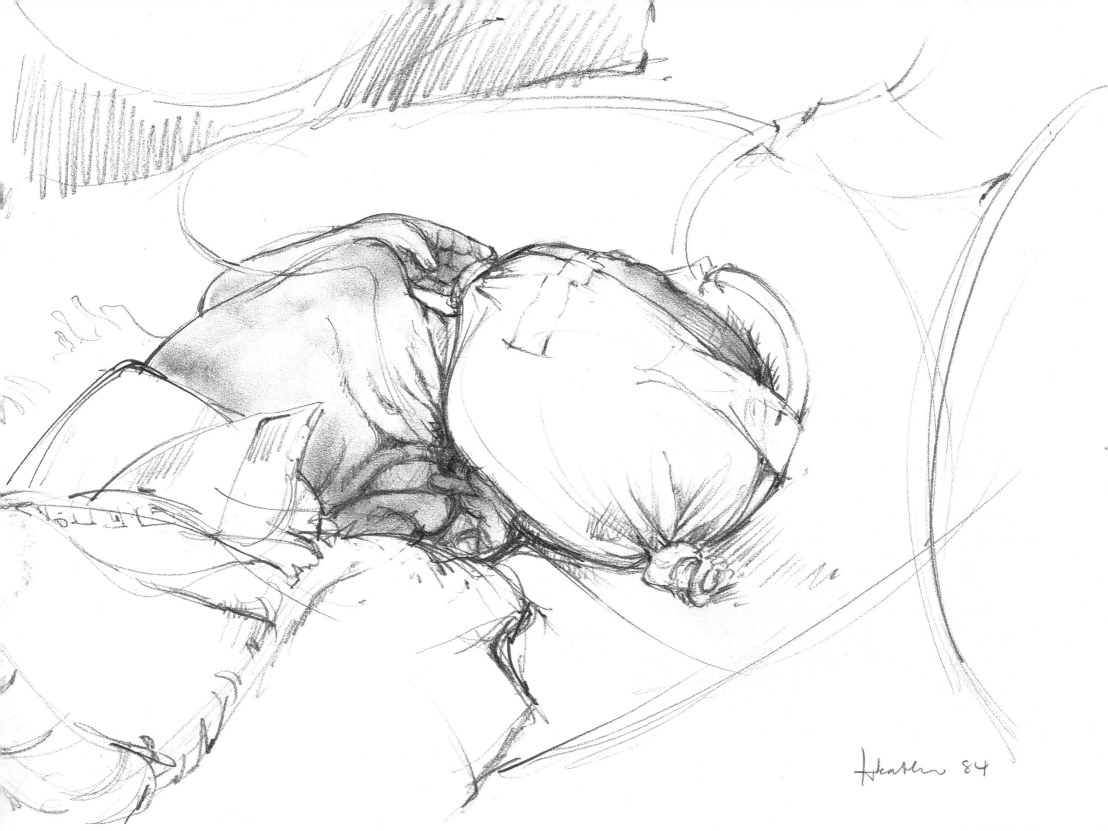

STUDIES OF RENÉ
1985. Pencil on white paper.
24 x 32 cm
Artist No. 761.

RENÉ
248

Heather 30/04/85

MIE
1984. Pencil on white paper.
24 x 32 cm
Artist No. 447.

MIE L.F.V.
450

Heather 84

STUDY, LIGHT-CHILD MAI
1984. Pencil on white paper.
24 x 32 cm
Artist No. 327.

EMIL. BABY IN A RESPIRATOR
1985. Pencil on white paper.
24 x 32 cm
Artist No. 626.

EMIL
135

theater
23/02/85

SOFIE, *PALATOSCHISIS*
1984. Pencil on white paper.
24 x 32 cm
(Original lost, reproduced from negative by Gert Jørgensen.)
Artist No. 333.

THOR
1984. Pencil on white paper.
21 x 29.7 cm
Artist No. 255.

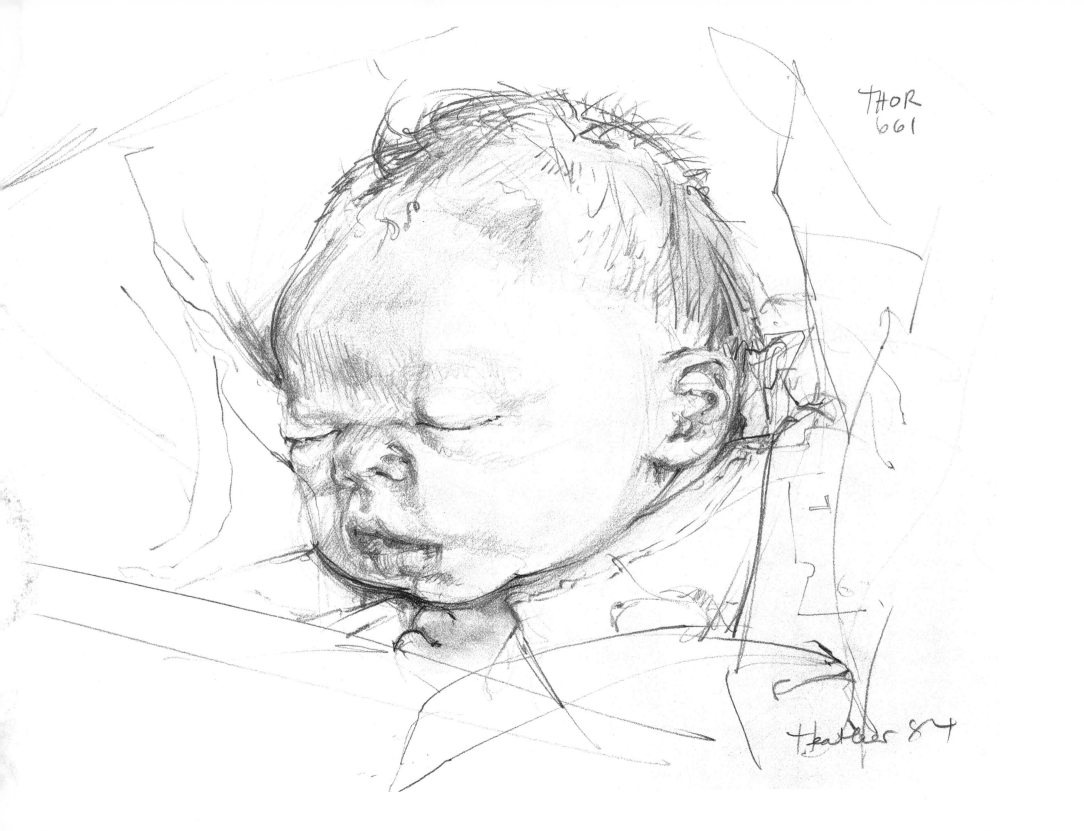

THOR
661

Heather 84

INCUBATOR DRAWING
1984. Pencil on white paper.
24 x 32 cm
Artist No. 267.

ANDERS (2)
1984. Pencil on white paper.
24 x 32 cm
Artist No. 476.

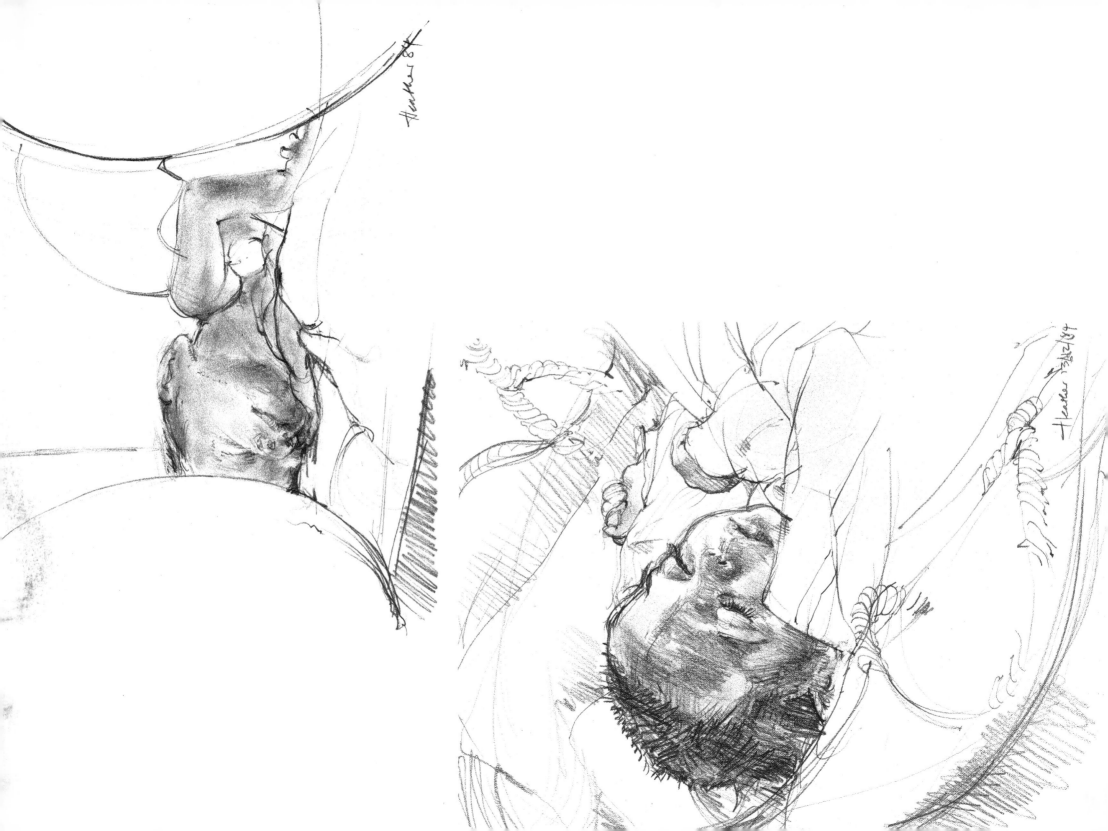

SALINA IN THE INCUBATOR
1984. Pencil on white paper.
24 x 32 cm
Collection Ulla Amsinck, Denmark.
Artist No. 436.

"MULLER" WITH WALKMAN
1985. Pencil on white paper.
24 x 32 cm
Collection Anny Madsen and Trond Bengtsen, Denmark.
Artist No. 773.

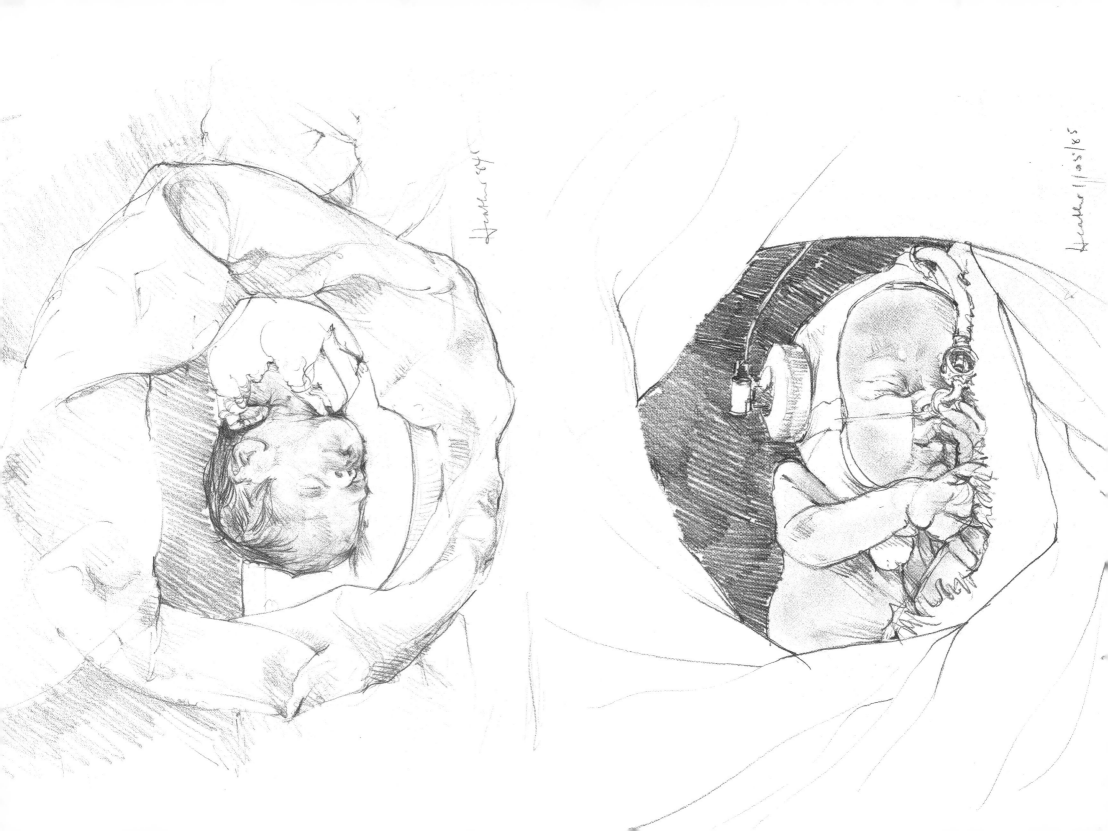

HENRIK, *MENINGITIS*
1985. Pencil on white paper.
24 x 32 cm
Artist No. 494.

DANIELL
1985. Pencil on white paper.
24 x 32 cm
Artist No. 525.

BABY AND FATHER
1984. Pencil on white paper.
24 x 32 cm
Collection Ursula Nielsen and Finn Petersen, Demark.
Artist No. 362.

MARIA, *PRAEMATUR*. INCUBATOR DRAWING
1985. Pencil on white paper.
24 x 32 cm
Artist No. 500.

MARIA '00

Apuli 12/2/95

NIELS CHRISTIAN
1985. Pencil on white paper.
24 x 32 cm
Collection Allan and Nobuko Hermansen, Denmark.
Artist No. 481.

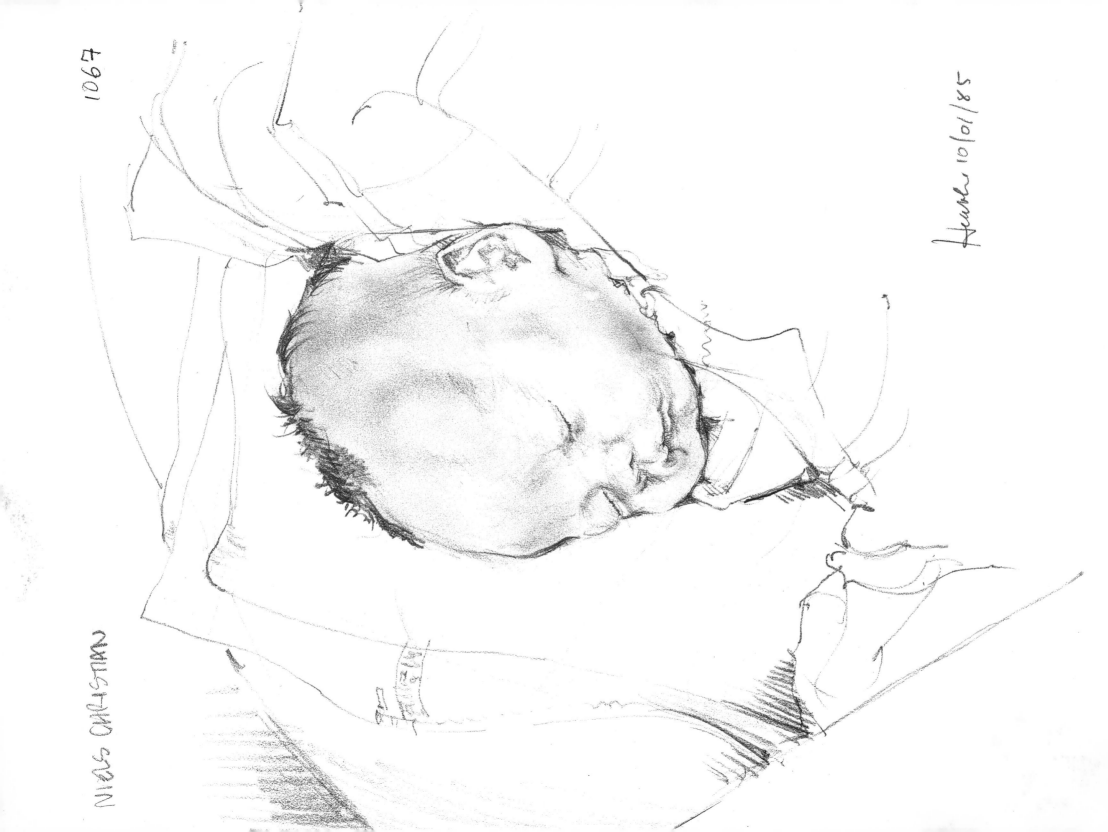

NIELS CHRISTIAN

1067

Huck 10/01/85

BENJAMIN, *HYPOGLYCAEMI*
1984. Pencil on white paper.
24 x 32 cm
Collection Alina and Fiszel Nusbaum, Denmark.
Artist No. 244.

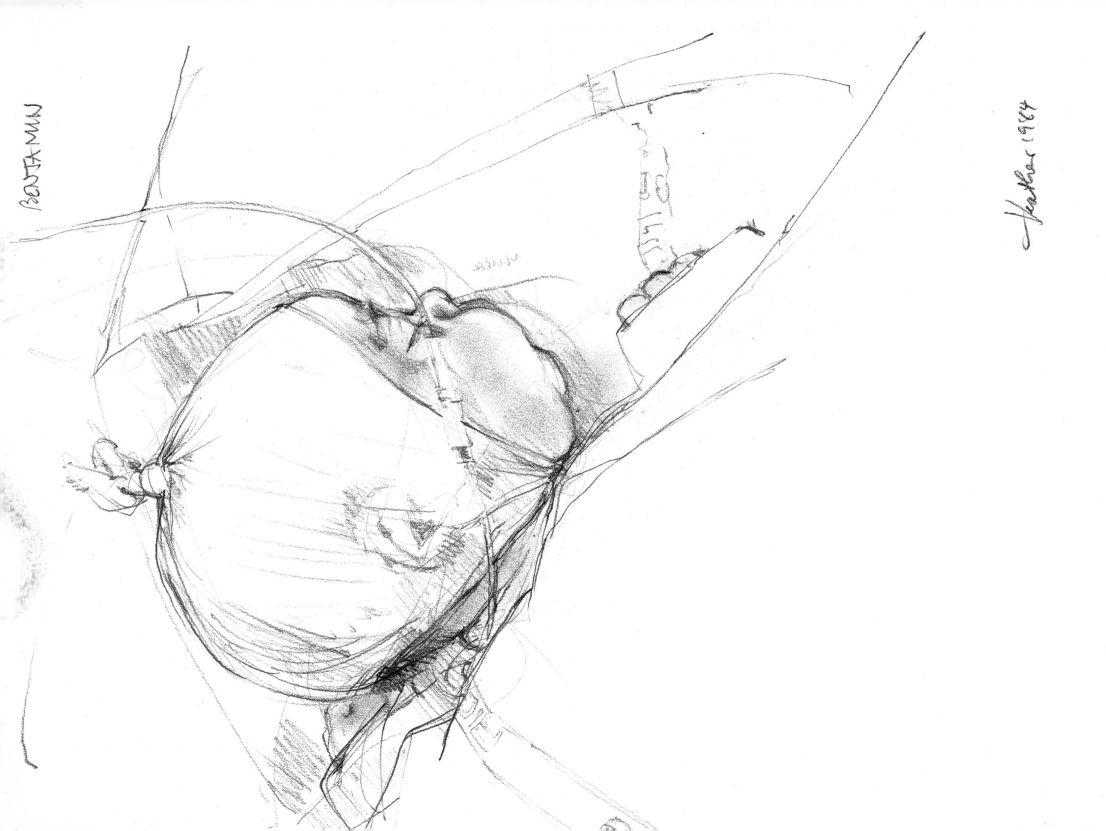

BENJAMIN

Heather 1984

RIKKE. HEAD OF BABY GIRL
1984. Pencil on white paper.
24 x 32 cm
Collection of Gertie Lauterbach and
Hans Verner Jensen, Denmark.
Artist No. 407.

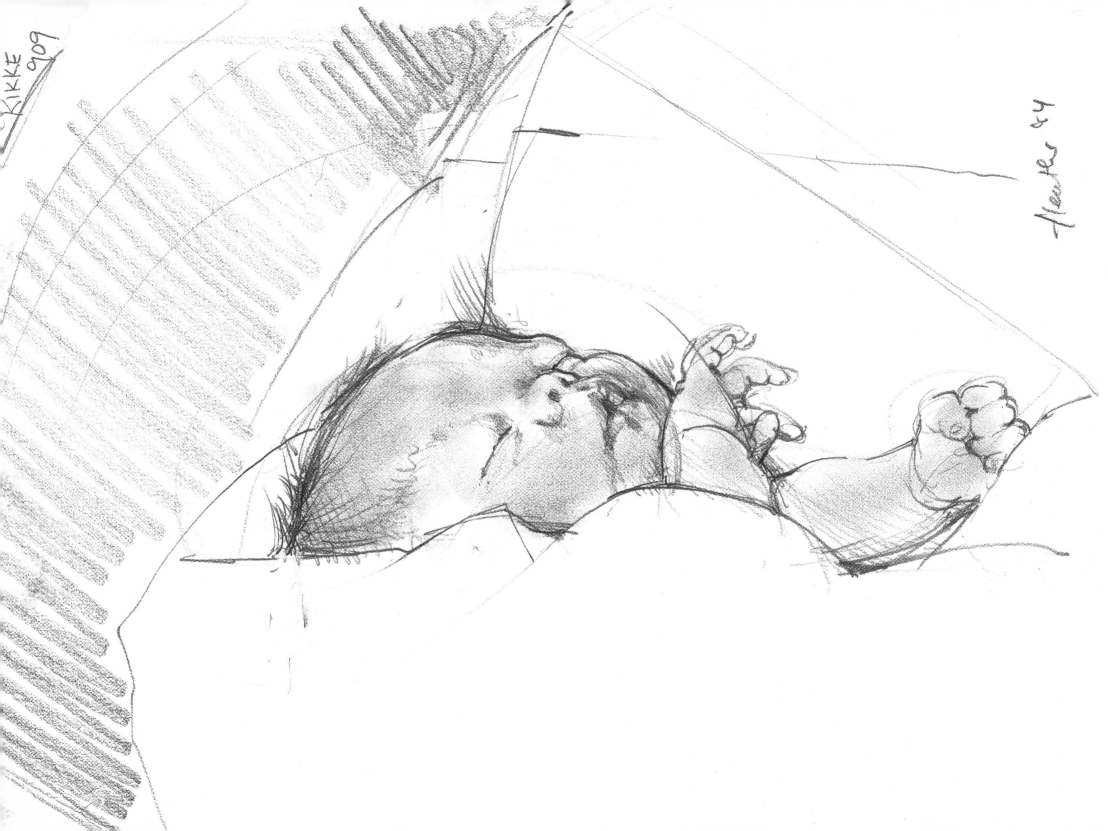

HAND STUDIES, MARIA EVA, 640 grams
(birth weight 700 grams).
1985. Pencil on white paper.
24 x 32 cm
Artist No. 784.

LIGHT-BOX BABY
1984. Pencil on white paper.
21 x 29.7 cm
Artist No. 248

NIKKI. INCUBATOR DRAWING
1985. Pencil on white paper.
24 x 32 cm
Artist No. 624.

SALINA DANCES (2)

STUDIES OF PREMATURE HANDS
1984. Pencil on white paper.
24 x 32 cm
Collection Rita Edwards, Canada.
Artist No. 399.

SALINA DANCES (3)

STUDIES OF PREMATURE HANDS
1984. Pencil on white paper.
24 x 32 cm
Artist No. 402.

STUDIES OF PREMATURE LEGS
1984. Pencil on white paper.
24 x 32 cm
Collection Annette Mester, Denmark.
Artist No. 405.

Saline dancers.

THE AFTERWORD

A MEDICAL AFTERWORD

BY JØRGEN PAULIN, M.D.
Rigshospitalet,
Copenhagen, Denmark

The purpose of this afterword is to answer the questions most frequently asked about premature babies and to give a brief explanation of medical terms that appear in the poems and drawings.

Rigshospitalet's GN 5024 is unique in Denmark in that it cares for not only premature infants and newborns, but also other infants needing intensive care, mostly surgical patients. The ward serves the entire country, caring for babies who cannot be helped elsewhere, and as Rigshospitalet serves as a "district hospital" for Greenland and the Faroe Islands, we receive babies from these distant places also. Finally the ward serves a local function for part of the Copenhagen area. The open ward has space for 25-30 patients, and consists of six open aisles or rooms, three for intensive care and three for normal care. It has its own laboratory facilities, but otherwise resembles any other intensive care ward in the world.

According to the World Health Organization's definition, "premature" means born before term, and is applied to babies born before the 37th completed week of gestation. Thirty-eight to forty weeks is full term. A low-weight baby has a birth weight of 2500 g or less (approximately 5½ lbs.).

Premature signs vary a great deal depending on the gestational age. The lower the age, the more characteristic the signs: a large head in proportion to body size; small trunk; short and fine limbs; skin thin, reddish and wrinkled; ears flat and soft; hair thin and fuzzy. Body functions are poorly developed, with problems in breathing, taking food, maintaining body temperature, balancing salt and water in the body, etc. Because such reflexes as swallowing and coughing are feeble, tubes for feeding and suctioning are needed intermittently. In all, the premature has just too few resources to manage on its own.

Respirators are used to help babies who cannot yet breathe on their own, and provide the correct pressure and amount of air to the lungs through a nasal-tracheal tube.

An incubator is a self-regulating box that supports the baby in an environment as much like that of the uterus as possible. It is made of plexiglass to permit intensive observation of the baby when necessary. The sides can be opened, but two cloth-covered windows on each side provide access without particular loss of heat and oxygen.

DETAILS IN THE DRAWINGS:

The drip, seen as a bandage on the head, provides fluid and medicine which cannot be given orally.

The three cords to the white plasters are electrodes pasted to the baby's chest to register heartbeat (ECG) on the scope above the bed or incubator.

The raised gray electrodes provide transcutaneous reading (through the skin) of oxygen and carbon dioxide ratios, and thus eliminate frequent blood tests.

The little bonnets, cut from tube gauze, help to keep the drip, eye mask or nasal tube in place.

While it was previously believed that premature babies needed quiet and isolation, we now know that they thrive best with stimulation. So the incubators become little worlds of coloured pictures, soft toys, mobiles and music. Some parents provide a walkman for their baby, as music and known voices seem to lessen the baby's stress.

"Light-children" is the term used for babies with jaundice. Lying naked on their beds, they are treated with 'daylight' light. Light-boxes provide light from beneath as well as from above, and the child lies on a transparent mattress. The masks protect the babies' eyes from the bright light.

MEDICAL TERMS THAT APPEAR IN POEMS OR DRAWINGS:

APNOE (APNEA) - interrupted breathing for several seconds; the baby usually responds to stimulus, such as touching; apnoe can result in cyanosis, a decrease in heart rate.

ASPHYXIA - condition that follows lack of oxygen at birth

DMM - Diabetes Mellitus Matris - mother has diabetes

FACE PRESENTATION - born face first

HB - Hyperbilirubinaemi - jaundice - "light-child"

HYDROCEPHALUS - water on the brain; treated by inserting a drain

HYPOGLYCAEMI - low blood sugar

LFV - *lav fodselvaegt* - low birth weight

MEC. ASP. - meconium aspiration; at birth baby inhaled birth fluid containing meconium (excrement)

NM - Narcomania Matris - mother addicted to drugs; the newborn also addicted, suffers withdrawal symptoms.

OESOPHAGUS ATRESI - part of oesophagus missing

PALATOSCHISIS - cleft palate

Rh IMM. - rhesus baby - jaundice - "light-child"

SFD - small for date/light for date - birth weight is under normal for the gestational age

STENO FALLOT - "Blue baby" - a heart malformation, where the blood contains insufficient oxygen

TVILLING A - first born twin

A NOTE ON THE AUTHOR

Heather Spears was born in 1934 in Vancouver, British Columbia, Canada. She is a graduate of the Vancouver School of Art, the University of British Columbia (1956), and the University of Copenhagen (1983). In 1956, while still living in Canada, she won an Emily Carr Scholarship for study abroad. In 1959 she married potter Leonard Goldenberg and is the mother of three sons. She has been a resident of Denmark since 1962 and lives on the island of Bornholm.

Heather is the author of three books of poetry: *Asylum Poems* (1959, Chapbook-Jay MacPherson), *The Danish Portraits* (1967, Ryerson Press), *From the Inside* (1972, Fiddlehead Poetry Books), and is a member of the League of Canadian Poets. Currently she works as a free-lance graphic artist and teacher of art in Denmark. In Scandinavia, her drawings have been widely exhibited in galleries and hospitals, and she has given many readings of poetry.

Since 1983 Heather Spears has concentrated her work on the drawing of newborn infants at Rigshospitalet in Copenhagen where she has become well-known to staff and parents. She has been travelling weekly to Copenhagen on the night ferry from Bornholm, biking over to the hospital about 11 p.m. There, in the neonatal ward, she has been drawing nightly for four to five hours. Using her talents, both as poet and graphic artist, she has here recorded the world of these special newborn infants, many of them premature.

The text of this edition of DRAWINGS FROM THE NEWBORN has been set in Garamond type on 100 lb. Japanese matt art paper. The title and dustjacket were set in Caslon.